21st
Century
Skills Library

REAL WORLD SCIENCE

ECOSYSTEMS

Stephen Currie

Cherry Lake Publishing
Ann Arbor, Michigan

CHERRY LAKE Publishing

Published in the United States of America by Cherry Lake Publishing
Ann Arbor, Michigan
www.cherrylakepublishing.com

Content Adviser: Laura Graceffa, middle school science teacher; BA degree in science, Vassar College; MA degrees in science and education, Brown University

Photo Credits: Cover and page 1, © MaxFX/Shutterstock; page 4, © Juriah Mosen/ Shutterstock; page 6, © Steve Estvanik/Shutterstock; page 8, © SJGH/Shutterstock; page 10, © groomee/Shutterstock; page 12, © Harry Hu/Shutterstock; page 14, © mashe/Shutterstock; page 16, © J. McPhail/Shutterstock; page 18, © Rusty Dodson/ Shutterstock; page 19, © Mariette Budel/Shutterstock; page 21, © Stephen Kerkhofs/ Shutterstock; page 22, © Dmitry Grivenko/Shutterstock; page 24, © Denis Blofield/ Shutterstock; page 25, © Stephanie Coffman/Shutterstock; page 26, © Andrew Williams/ Shutterstock

Library of Congress Cataloging-in-Publication Data

Currie, Stephen, 1960-
Ecosystems / Stephen Currie.
  p. cm. —(Real world science)
ISBN-13: 978-1-60279-458-0
ISBN-10: 1-60279-458-8
1. Biotic communities—Juvenile literature. I. Title. II. Series.

QH541.14.C87 2009
577—dc22   2008049662

Cherry Lake Publishing would like to acknowledge the work of
The Partnership for 21st Century Skills.
Please visit www.21stcenturyskills.org *for more information.*

TABLE OF CONTENTS

CHAPTER ONE

THE WEB OF LIFE

Red and blue macaws perch on a branch in the South American rain forest.

Welcome aboard! Today's tour will bring you to exciting places across the globe, all of them filled with living things. The first stop is the South American rain forest. You'll notice that the air is hot and damp, and the trees are enormous. Their branches almost block the sunlight. Don't you love the brightly colored birds? Wait! Is that a *snake*?

Moving on! Now we're in the tundra, a flat, cold land near the Arctic. Notice that there are hardly any trees—just low grass and a few other plants. Did you see that white fox running by? Try not to step in that pond. The water's *freezing*. Whoa! Is that a *polar bear*?

Next stop is a drop of water! Yes, there's life here, too. Those things drifting by are microorganisms, or tiny living things. Yes, some of them are eating each other. That's the way things work in drops of water—like everywhere else on the planet. It's a microorganism-eat-microorganism world. Fasten your seat belts. Home we go!

It might seem that rain forests, tundra, and drops of water have nothing in common. But they are alike in one important way. All of them are ecosystems. An ecosystem is a community of living things in the same area. Ecosystems also include things in the area that are not alive. Scientists often describe an ecosystem as a biological

"neighborhood."

There are many kinds of ecosystems in the world. Do you live near a

river? A river ecosystem includes the fish in the river. It includes raccoons and

other animals that eat the fish. And it includes the plants at the water's edge.

Water is not alive. But it's a part of a river ecosystem, too. How cold is

the water? How deep is it? How fast does it flow? All of these can make the

river a good or a bad place for different living things to call home.

Water is an important part of this pond's ecosystem.

The desert is another well-known ecosystem.

Deserts are dry. They have few trees. Often, they

are hot, and they are usually rocky or sandy.

Still, deserts are home to many different

species, or types, of animals and plants. Camels

are part of some desert ecosystems. So are snakes.

Desert plants include cactus and sagebrush.

Sand, rocks, and weather are part of the

ecosystem of a desert, too.

All the species in an ecosystem are connected.

"Plants and animals do not exist independently,"

writes one author. "Their lives are closely bound

up with other plants and animals." Whatever

Suppose you wanted to teach younger children about ecosystems. Design a simple game that would help children learn about deserts, wetlands, rain forests, and two or three other ecosystems of your choice. Think about the kinds of animals and plants that live in these ecosystems. Think also about the kind of land and the kind of weather each ecosystem might have. Some possible designs for a game:

- Make cards that show different ecosystems and different animals that live in them. Players have to match the cards in some way.

- Make a game board with a start and a finish. The players have to roll a number cube or draw cards to move forward. The spaces show different ecosystems. Different things can happen in each space, which either slows players down or speeds them up.

A frog waits on a lily pad for its mosquito meal to fly by.

happens to one species in an ecosystem can affect all the others. Wetlands are a good example of how species use each other.

In wetlands, the land is swampy and the air is moist. Species in a wetlands ecosystem might include frogs, mosquitoes, and lily pads.

If you've visited a wetland, you might have seen frogs sitting on lily pads. What are they doing? They're waiting for mosquitoes to fly by! When the mosquitoes come near, they flick out their tongues and eat them. The lily pads provide the frogs with a place to catch their dinner. The mosquitoes *are* the dinner. So, all three of these species are connected.

REAL WORLD SCIENCE CHALLENGE

This table gives weather information for three American cities. Each city is in or near a different kind of ecosystem. Fairbanks, Alaska, is on the tundra. Tucson, Arizona, is in the desert. And New Orleans, Louisiana, is near wetlands. "Precipitation" includes mostly rainfall. "Relative humidity" tells how wet or dry the air is. The higher the number, the wetter the air. "Annual" means for a year. So, the "average annual snowfall" tells how much it snows in a year. Look closely at the table. See if you can figure out which city is which.

City	Average Temperature in January	Average Temperature in July	Average Annual Precipitation	Average Annual Snowfall	Average Relative Humidity (Morning)
?	52° F/11°C	87° F/31°C	11.7 in/297 mm	1.3 in/33 mm	52%
?	53° F/12°C	82° F/28°C	61.6 in/1565 mm	0 in/0 mm	88%
?	-8° F/-22°C	62° F/17°C	10.7 in/272 mm	70.1 in/1781 mm	74%

[Information comes from Weatherbase, www.weatherbase.com/weather/state.php3?c=US&s=&refer=]

(Turn to page 29 for the answer)

No matter how big or small an ecosystem is, every ecosystem has connections like these. The connections help make each ecosystem a unique part of the earth.

CHAPTER TWO

COMPETITION AND SURVIVAL

Brightly colored flowers provide nectar for bees.

Have you ever acted in a play? Actors often have to compete for a part. When you compete, you try to be better than someone else at whatever you're doing.

Say that 20 people want to be in a play. But there are only 12 parts. Then those 20 people must compete for those 12 parts. The actors who get the parts win the competition.

Animals and plants don't put on plays. But they do compete with each other. Every ecosystem has **resources**. Resources are things that plants or animals use to live and grow. Air is a resource. Food and water are resources, too.

Sometimes, an ecosystem has lots of one kind of resource. Then, every species can get what it needs. Ocean ecosystems have enough water to support many kinds of fish, for example. And forests have plenty of air for trees.

But more often, the resources in an ecosystem are limited. Sunlight is a resource. It helps trees grow strong and healthy. Tall trees with straight trunks stick out above other trees. So, they get plenty of sunlight. Shorter trees don't get as much. They're in the shade of their taller neighbors. So,

Sometimes, two species in an ecosystem have a special relationship. In this relationship, each species behaves in a way that helps the other. One example is bees and flowers. Flowers make a substance called pollen. In order to reproduce, a flower has to get its pollen to another flower. But flowers can't move, which makes that hard. Luckily, bees are attracted to certain flowers. They land on these flowers to eat or drink foods that the flowers produce. When they are done eating, they fly off. But the bees take something else with them. Some of the pollen on these flowers sticks to their feet. When the bees fly to another flower, the pollen comes off. It allows the flowers to reproduce. So, both the bees and the flowers benefit.

Tall trees like these win the competition for sunlight.

tree species that grow tall win the competition for sunlight. They are more

likely to be strong and healthy.

Animals compete, too. They compete for shelter, or places to live. They

also compete for food. Some species win the competition by pushing other

animals out of their way, like squirrels at a bird feeder.

Some species have other advantages. The crested lizard lives in the

desert. It copes very well with heat. On extremely hot days, crested

lizards are the only animals out looking for food. On these days, writes one scientist, the lizard "has no competition, and can claim for itself

all the food it can find."

REAL WORLD SCIENCE CHALLENGE

You can use a deck of cards to show how different species compete. In this game, the black cards stand for one species of animal. The red cards stand for another species. The species are competing for shelter. Put the spades and hearts into a pile. Shuffle those cards. Deal out seven cards at random— that is, without looking at them first. There will be more of one color. Let's say there are more reds. That means the red animals are doing better at finding shelter than the black ones. Take one of the spades away. Add a diamond (another red card) to the pile. Now, shuffle the pile again. Deal out seven more cards. Add a new card of the color that won. Take away a card of the color that lost. What happens?

(Turn to page 29 for the answer)

If you compete for a part in a play and you don't get it, you'll be

disappointed. But losing a competition is far more serious for an animal

or a plant. After all, if birds can't find food or shelter, they may not survive.

So, competition can mean life or death.

Plants grow more easily when earthworms (pictured) dig through soil.

Some species help each other compete. The earthworms in a forest

ecosystem are an example. When earthworms dig through the forest

soil, says one scientist, they "improve the soil structure, improve water

movement through the soil, [and] improve plant root growth." All these

changes give plants more resources. So, earthworms make it easier for

plants to grow in the forest.

But that's not all. Earthworms help animals, too. How? First, earthworms are food for some birds and other animals. Besides, if there are more plants, then there is more food for plant-eating animals in the ecosystem.

Better soil helps trees grow, too. Many birds and other animals build homes on branches or in hollow parts of trees. When there are more trees, there's more space for these animals to live.

The living things in an ecosystem are always competing. But whether they know it or not, they are always working together, too.

Choose an ecosystem that interests you, such as a wetland, a meadow, or a desert. Think about the resources this ecosystem can provide. List a few.

Then, think about how different animals can find and use these resources. What characteristics will be most helpful for finding food, energy, and shelter in this ecosystem? For instance, animals lose body heat through their ears. Animals that live in a cold climate often have small ears, so they will lose less heat on chilly days. But an animal that lives in the desert might have big ears. Big ears give off more heat.

Now, sketch an animal from your imagination. Label the features that will help this animal compete in the ecosystem you chose. Describe how the features will help it survive.

CHAPTER THREE

PRODUCERS AND CONSUMERS

A field mouse looks for seeds and berries in a meadow.

A mouse is running through a meadow looking for food. Luckily, the ground is covered with berries. Berries are easy to eat. They help mice grow and stay healthy.

But what the mouse doesn't know is that a hungry snake is just a few feet away. The snake waits and watches. Before long the mouse moves just a little too close. Snap! Now the mouse isn't eating lunch any more.

Instead, the mouse *is* lunch!

The mouse, the snake, and the berries are part of a food chain. Food

chains describe what different species eat in an ecosystem. In this example,

snakes eat mice and mice eat berries. You can sketch a food chain like this:

berries → mice → snakes.

REAL WORLD SCIENCE CHALLENGE

Choose one of the following ecosystems: desert, rain forest, or ocean. Use library resources or the Internet to find out about the animals and plants that live in this ecosystem. Then create a food chain that shows how some of these animals and plants are connected. Draw and label the living things in the chain. Finally, draw arrows between them. Point the arrows away from the plant or animal that is being eaten so the arrows show how energy is being passed up the food chain. What did you put at the beginning of your food chain? What's in the middle? What's at the end?

(Turn to page 29 for the answer)

All food chains have something in common. They begin with

a plant. Plants take energy from the sun. They turn the energy into food.

Plants are called producers because they produce, or make, food. Berry

bushes are one kind of producer.

Like other snakes, a milksnake is a consumer in the food chain.

Animals are **consumers**. That is, they eat other things. Some consumers

eat only plants. Others eat only animals. Some eat both. The energy in

the berries travels up the food chain to the consumers. First, it goes to the

mouse. Then it goes to the snake.

There are also organisms called **decomposers**. To decompose means to

break something down. Decomposers break dead things into bits. Those bits go back into the soil. Mushrooms are decomposers. Some kinds of bacteria are decomposers, too.

Every ecosystem has lots of different food chains. Food chains go together to form a food web. Food webs include *all* the things that an animal eats. Snakes eat mice. But they also eat rats, small birds, and some kinds of insects. A food web shows all of these connections.

Food webs connect all species in an ecosystem. In the ocean near Antarctica, for instance, killer whales are connected to tiny one-celled organisms called diatoms. How? The killer whales eat

Mushrooms help create soil by breaking down dead things.

seals. Seals eat fish. Fish eat small shrimp-like animals called krill. And krill

eat diatoms. Even things that never eat each other are connected.

REAL WORLD SCIENCE CHALLENGE

Get permission from an adult before you try this experiment. Once you have permission, take a vegetable or a piece of fruit, such as a celery stalk or a strawberry. Place it outside. Cover it with a strainer so that large animals can't get to it, and so it can get fresh air.

Every morning, check the food. How does it look? Has it changed color? Has it changed shape? Is it smaller than it once was? Or has it gotten bigger? Is there a smell? Record your observations. (Be sure to wash your hands if you've touched the food.)

Throw the food out when it becomes too disgusting to look at any more. How long did that take? What role did decomposers play in this process? Wash the strainer carefully. Then repeat with a piece of cheese and again with a piece of bread. How do these foods change? Why?

(Turn to page 29 for the answer)

Because everything in a food web is connected, anything that happens

to one species affects other species, too. Today, there are fewer sharks in

some parts of the world than there used to be. Sharks like to eat a kind of fish called a ray. So, there are more rays today in places where the sharks have been disappearing.

Rays such as this spotted eagle ray provide food for sharks.

Still, what's good for one kind of animal isn't always good for nature. Rays eat sea creatures called scallops. Once, North Carolina had lots of scallops. "You couldn't set a foot down without stepping on three of them," says a fisherman. But the scallops are disappearing. Without sharks, there are so many rays that they gobble up the scallops one after the other.

Food webs have developed over thousands of years. It's best for ecosystems if they stay the way they are.

CHAPTER FOUR

ENDANGERED AND EXTINCT

When people built farms and towns on grasslands, black-footed ferrets almost died out.

The black-footed ferret is a small animal that lives on prairies, or grasslands. Once there were plenty of black-footed ferrets in the American West. But by 1987, there were only 16 black-footed ferrets in the whole world. The ferrets were almost **extinct**. When a species is extinct, there are no more of its kind anywhere on earth.

Part of the problem was disease. But the problem also had to do with the ferrets' **habitat**, or where they lived. People were digging up grasslands to build farms and towns. "In some areas," says a Web site about ferrets, "up to 99 percent of the prairie has been destroyed." When their habitat was gone, the ferrets could not find homes. They began to die out.

REAL WORLD SCIENCE CHALLENGE

Here are some well-known endangered animals: the gray wolf; the Siberian tiger; the California condor; and the Indian elephant. Choose one of these animals. Use library resources or the Internet to learn more about them. Then answer the following questions:

• What ecosystems are home to your animal?

• What changes to the ecosystem hurt the animal? Which changes could help it? Why?

• What other changes are making it hard for the animal to survive?

• Suppose you were in charge of making sure the animal did not become extinct. How would you try to save it? What problems would there be in putting your plan into action?

(Turn to page 29 for the answer)

Luckily, scientists were able to help. They brought the ferrets to places where the prairie had not been torn up. Today, there are more than 1,000 black-footed ferrets in North America. That's the good news.

Habitat destruction threatens these river turtles. Many turtle species are in trouble.

The bad news is that many other species are also endangered, or close to being extinct.

Species become endangered in different ways. Lots of living things die when people damage the ecosystems where they make their homes. This is especially true for plants. It is also a big problem for animals in ponds and lakes. Turtles are a good example. They cannot easily move to a new home if their ecosystem is destroyed. Some scientists think that one-third of the world's turtle species are in trouble.

Hunting is a problem, too. American grasslands once were covered with bison, also called buffalo. "To count them is almost impossible," wrote an explorer. Then, people hunted them until they were almost extinct.

Climate change is another concern. Polar bears hunt and rest on big sheets of ice. But the Arctic is getting warmer. There is less ice than there used to be. If the Arctic keeps warming up, the ice may vanish. That would harm the polar bears. It might even make them extinct.

Bison were hunted almost to extinction. Now they are protected.

Hemlock, which provides shade for some river fish, is dying out in some places.

It's always sad when an animal or a plant is gone forever. But extinction isn't just sad. It's a big problem for the environment. When one species disappears, the ecosystem is no longer in balance. Animals that eat the endangered species may be in serious trouble. And extinctions hurt species in other ways, too.

In parts of Kentucky, for instance, hemlock trees are dying out. Hemlock trees provide shade. The shade keeps streams and rivers cool.

When trees die, the water heats up. Some fish cannot survive in the warmer water. Then, they die, too.

People can help protect ecosystems. They can try to destroy as little habitat as possible. They can learn more about how animals and plants are connected. They can help species that are in trouble.

REAL WORLD SCIENCE CHALLENGE

Choose an ecosystem near your home or school. You might choose a forest or a stream. You could also choose a city park, a backyard, or even a puddle. Look closely at the ecosystem you choose. What does it look like? What sounds do you hear? How does it smell? What are the plants? Are there animals? What kinds? What nonliving things could be important?

Take careful notes on what you see and hear. Write down words and phrases that describe the ecosystem you chose. Draw simple pictures, too. Then make some guesses about how the plants and animals in the ecosystem are connected.

Come back in two or three days. Study the ecosystem again. Has anything changed? What? How has it changed?

(Turn to page 29 for the answer)

Several kinds of birds once lived on the Pacific island of Guam. Many of these species are now extinct. The brown tree snake is the cause. The snakes ate so many birds and bird eggs that the birds died out.

The brown tree snake is not native to Guam. It arrived on ships carrying people and cargo in the 1950s. No one meant for there to be brown tree snakes in Guam. It just happened. And when it happened, it threw Guam's ecosystem out of balance.

The brown tree snakes on Guam are an invasive species. Invasive species are animals or plants that move to a new place and take over. They can throw an ecosystem out of balance. Many invasive species exist around the world. Often, they destroy other living things. And like the tree snakes, they can even make other wildlife extinct.

And they can remember that all living things are important in nature. Destroying even one species can cause problems for a whole ecosystem—maybe the whole world. As one writer says, "The balance of nature is delicate but essential for life."

REAL WORLD SCIENCE CHALLENGE ANSWERS

Chapter One
Page 9

High snowfall figures and low temperatures show that Fairbanks is the third city. It's harder to tell New Orleans (wetlands) from Tucson (desert). The second city has higher humidity and much more rain, so it's a wetter place. That fits a wetland. So the first city is a desert. Answers: Top = Tucson; middle = New Orleans; bottom = Fairbanks.

Chapter Two
Page 13

The "winning" species in each round increases its numbers by adding a new card. This shows what happens when a species gets what it needs: its population grows. The losing species in each round loses a card—it begins to disappear. Once a species starts to win, it is more and more likely to win, just as would happen in real life. The game will end soon afterward. This shows the extinction or moving away of the losing species.

Chapter Three
Page 17

Your food chain should start with a plant. There should also be at least two or three animals. If you did a forest food chain, for instance, you could include nuts, then squirrels, then foxes, and maybe hawks or wolves at the end.

Page 20

You might discover that the food becomes very hard or very soft in just a few days. There's a good chance that it will change color or shape. Most foods will get smaller as the water inside them dries up. Many foods may begin to smell bad too, and you might see white stuff called mold begin to grow on them. Most of the process is carried out by bacteria. However, different foods break down in different ways and at different speeds. Some fruits go bad very quickly. Some kinds of bread may take longer. And some kinds of cheese may stay fresh on the inside for a very long time, even if they go bad on the surface.

Chapter Four
Page 23

Changes to the ecosystem affect the populations of all these animals. Habitat loss might be an especially big problem. Other factors might be important, too. Don't be surprised if you find that your solutions to the problem seem expensive, or if you think that people won't like them very much for other reasons. You might even wonder if your solutions could really work. Unfortunately, that's the way things are. In real life, it's hard to save endangered species.

Page 27

You probably noticed a lot of different things. If you chose a park, for example, you might have heard the cries of birds and smelled the scent of freshly cut grass. You might have seen animals like squirrels, bugs, or crows. And you probably saw bushes, trees, and a few flowers. One possible connection between species in the park might be "The birds could eat the bugs." If you visit the same park a few days later, you might see leaves changing color, or plants growing taller, or maybe even a few more of one kind of animal.

GLOSSARY

consumer (kun SOO mer) an animal that eats animals or plants

decomposers (dee kum POHZ erz) living things that break down the bodies of other forms of life that have died

endangered (en DAIN jurd) scarce or rare, and threatened with becoming extinct

extinct (eks TINKT) no longer in existence; used to describe a species

food chain a description of which species eats which other species, showing how energy is transferred from one species to another

food web a group of food chains in a single ecosystem

habitat (HABB i tat) the natural place where an animal or plant lives

microorganisms (MY crow OR guh nizmz) simple forms of life too small to be seen except under a microscope

producers (pro DOO surz) living things that make their own food and energy; plants

resources (REE sore siz) things that animals and plants can use to grow and live, such as shelter, food, and air

species (SPEE shees) type of plant or animal

FOR MORE INFORMATION

Books

Gritzner, Charles F. *The Tropics.* New York: Chelsea House, 2006.

Johansson, Philip. *Marshes and Swamps: A Wetland Web of Life.* Berkeley Heights, NJ: Enslow, 2008.

Kessler, Colleen. *Hands-on Ecology: Real-Life Activities for Kids.* Waco, TX: Prufrock, 2006.

Sohn, Emily. *The Environment.* New York: Chelsea Clubhouse, 2006.

Spilsbury, Louise and Richard. *The War in Your Backyard: Life in an Ecosystem.* Chicago: Raintree, 2006.

Web Resources

Ecokids
www.ecokidsonline.com/pub/index.cfm
Activities and information about the environment that includes plenty of useful resources for further study of ecosystems

Geography4Kids.com, "Biosphere"
www.geography4kids.com/files/land_intro.html
Links and data about the world and its ecosystems that includes information on food chains and food webs

Missouri Botanical Garden, "What's It Like Where You Live?"
www.mbgnet.net/
Information and links about ecosystems and nature in general

U.S. Environmental Protection Agency, "Ecosystems"
www.epa.gov/students/ecosystems.htm
Facts about the ecosystems of the world written for students, with many links to activities and further information

INDEX

ABOUT THE AUTHOR

Stephen Currie is a writer and a teacher who is the author of many books. He lives with his family in New York State, where he enjoys kayaking, snowshoeing, and hiking.